MW00414970

To:

From:

Inspired by You

Penguin Random House LLC
1745 Broadway
New York, New York 10014
penguinrandomhouse.com

This volume first published 2019

First published by Guided Journals, an imprint of
Penguin Random House LLC, 2019

ISBN: 9780593196526

Printed in the United States of America
1 3 5 7 9 10 8 6 4 2

Cover and Interior Design by: Meredith Snyder
Cover Image by: Wikki/Shutterstock.com

Dear Educator,

Inspired by You is designed to help **you** build a **positive mindset**, express your **creativity**, get the most out of your busy day, and **give the best to your students**. In this journal, you'll find **motivational quotes**, questions for **personal reflection**, thought-provoking **list prompts**, a **calendar** to help set goals, as well as plenty of space to **brainstorm, sketch, and jot down new ideas**. Keep it on hand for whenever inspiration strikes and **don't be afraid to make it your own!**

Want to share your own *Inspired by You* journey on social media? Snap a photo of your lists, drawings, or plans and tag **#inspiredbyyoujournal** to join the conversation and inspire other educators.

Thanks for all **you** do.

"There's nothing that can help you understand your beliefs more than trying to explain them to an inquisitive child."

⟆ Frank A. Clark

When did you realize you wanted to be an educator?

....

....

....

....

....

....

....

....

....

....

....

....

....

....

....

What is your favorite aspect of teaching?

_____

_____

_____

_____

_____

_____

_____

_____

_____

_____

_____

_____

_____

_____

_____

"Children have never been very good at listening to adults but they have never failed to imitate them."
— James Baldwin

"Kindness to children, love for children, goodness to children — these are the only investments that never fail."

— Henry David Thoreau

List 5 reasons why you became a teacher.

1. ....

2. ....

3. ....

4. ....

5. ....

In what ways has teaching been what you expected?

....

....

....

....

....

....

....

....

....

....

....

....

....

....

....

....

List 5 things for which you feel grateful.

1. ....

2. ....

3. ....

4. ....

5. ....

What is one of your most treasured childhood memories at school? Why does it feel special?

....

....

....

....

....

....

....

....

....

....

....

....

....

....

....

....

"The path of development is a journey of discovery that is clear only in retrospect, and it's rarely a straight line."
— Eileen Kennedy-Moore

List 5 of your favorite classroom activities.

1. ....

2. ....

3. ....

4. ....

5. ....

In what ways has teaching surprised you?

....

....

....

....

....

....

....

....

....

....

....

....

....

....

....

....

What is one thing you're glad to have learned over the past year?

"The real voyage of discovery consists not in seeking new landscapes, but in having new eyes."
— Marcel Proust

List 5 things in your classroom you couldn't teach without.

1. ....

2. ....

3. ....

4. ....

5. ....

List 5 people who have supported you, in ways big or small, along the way.

1. ....

2. ....

3. ....

4. ....

5. ....

What is one thing your students did that brought you joy in the past week?

_____

_____

_____

_____

_____

_____

_____

_____

_____

_____

_____

_____

_____

_____

_____

"Against the assault of laughter nothing can stand."
— Mark Twain

List 5 people you'd love to visit your classroom and speak to your students.

1. ....

2. ....

3. ....

4. ....

5. ....

What is one place that makes you feel calm?

....

....

....

....

....

....

....

....

....

....

....

....

....

....

....

Close your eyes for a minute and listen. What are the sounds you hear? How do they make you feel?

....

....

....

....

....

....

....

....

....

....

....

....

....

....

"Children see magic because they look for it."
— Christopher Moore

"A day is
Eternity's seed,
and we are its
Gardeners."

⸎ Erika Harris

List 5 ways that you can treat yourself this year.

1. ....

2. ....

3. ....

4. ....

5. ....

List 5 books you would like to read this year.

1. ....

2. ....

3. ....

4. ....

5. ....

What is one thing that makes you feel fulfilled?

If you could plan a weekend staycation without any obligations, what would you do?

....

....

....

....

....

....

....

....

....

....

....

....

....

....

....

....

"How beautiful it is to do nothing, and then rest afterward."
— Spanish proverb

List 5 times a student said or did something that made you laugh.

1. ....

2. ....

3. ....

4. ....

5. ....

List 5 things to look forward to during the year.

1. ....

2. ....

3. ....

4. ....

5. ....

If you could visit any place in the world on vacation, where would you go? Why?

....

....

....

....

....

....

....

....

....

....

....

....

....

....

....

....

"All life is an experiment. The more experiments you make, the better."
— Ralph Waldo Emerson

List 5 things that make you feel relaxed.

1. ....

2. ....

3. ....

4. ....

5. ....

List 5 ways to deal with frustration.

1. ....

2. ....

3. ....

4. ....

5. ....

What motivates you to learn and grow?

"Life is like riding a bicycle. To keep your balance, you must keep moving."
— Albert Einstein

"No one has yet fully realized the wealth of sympathy, kindness and generosity hidden in the soul of a child. The effort of every true education should be to unlock that treasure."

— Emma Goldman

List 5 things your students need.

(They don't have to be tangible.)

1. ....

2. ....

3. ....

4. ....

5. ....

What is your most prized possession?

"You can learn many things from children.
How much patience you have, for instance."
— Franklin P. Jones

How do your friends and/or family show their support to you? How do you show them your support?

....

....

....

....

....

....

....

....

....

....

....

....

....

....

....

....

"Only surround yourself with people who will lift you higher."
— Oprah Winfrey

List 5 things you would tell a friend who is having a bad day.

(Save this list and reread it if you have a bad day.)

1. ....

2. ....

3. ....

4. ....

5. ....

List 5 things you are excited about for the next school year.

1. ....

2. ....

3. ....

4. ....

5. ....

Think back on a time you were really proud of yourself. What made that achievement feel special?

....

....

....

....

....

....

....

....

....

....

....

....

....

....

....

....

"Who shall set a limit to the influence of a human being?"
— Ralph Waldo Emerson

"A sense of humor gets you through just about anything."

— Julia Louis-Dreyfus

List 5 epic fails you've experienced that made you laugh.

1. ....

2. ....

3. ....

4. ....

5. ....

What would you like to accomplish for yourself in the next five years?

....

....

....

....

....

....

....

....

....

....

....

....

....

....

....

....

"This day will not come again. Each minute is worth a priceless gem."
— Takuan Soho

"The success of love is in the loving—it is not in the result of loving. Of course it is natural in love to want the best for the other person, but whether it turns out that way or not does not determine the value of what we have done."

— Mother Teresa

List 5 lessons you hope your students will take away with them at the end of the school year.

1. ....

2. ....

3. ....

4. ....

5. ....

List 5 of your favorite books to use in the classroom.

1. ....

2. ....

3. ....

4. ....

5. ....

If a colleague asked you for a book recommendation, what would you immediately recommend? Why?

What's one thing you've wanted to try, but never have? Is there anything stopping you?

....

....

....

....

....

....

....

....

....

....

....

....

....

....

....

....

"Yesterday is gone. Tomorrow has not yet come. We have only today. Let us begin."
— Anonymous

List 5 songs that make you want to dance.

1. ....

2. ....

3. ....

4. ....

5. ....

List 5 things you want to improve at your school.

1. ....

2. ....

3. ....

4. ....

5. ....

What is one lesson you have learned from your students?

....

....

....

....

....

....

....

....

....

....

....

....

....

....

....

"It would be difficult to exaggerate the degree to which we are influenced by those we influence."
— Eric Hoffer

"Love the moment, and the energy of that moment will spread beyond all boundaries."

— Sister Corita Kent

List 5 moments you felt you made an impact on your students.

1. ....

2. ....

3. ....

4. ....

5. ....

When you look back at this time in your life, what do you hope to see?

"The things you do for yourself are gone when you are gone, but the things you do for others remain as your legacy."
— Kalu Kalu

"Don't try to be perfect; just be an excellent example of being human."

—Anthony Robbins

List 5 teaching challenges you have overcome.

1. ....

2. ....

3. ....

4. ....

5. ....

What are some things you might do to encourage your students? How can you use those same things to encourage yourself?

....

....

....

....

....

....

....

....

....

....

....

....

....

....

....

"Kids go where there is excitement. They stay where there is love."
— Zig Ziglar

Look back at the last list. List 5 things you learned from those experiences.

1. ....

2. ....

3. ....

4. ....

5. ....

List 5 ways you can improve your students lives.

1. ....

2. ....

3. ....

4. ....

5. ....

What kind of legacy would you like to build for younger generations?

....

....

....

....

....

....

....

....

....

....

....

....

....

....

....

....

"Children are our immortality; in them we see the story of our life written in a fairer hand."
— Alfred North Whitehead

List 5 lunches you wish your cafeteria served.

1. ....

2. ....

3. ....

4. ....

5. ....

If you could grab ice cream with anyone in the world, who would it be? Why?

....

....

....

....

....

....

....

....

....

....

....

....

....

....

....

....

....

Who is someone you truly admire, and why?
(If you can, let them know!)

"The degree of loving is measured by the degree of giving."
— Edwin Louis Cole

Think of your biggest mentor and list 5 of their best traits.

1. ....

2. ....

3. ....

4. ....

5. ....

Who makes you laugh most often?

....

....

....

....

....

....

....

....

....

....

....

....

....

....

....

....

"Tell me and I forget, teach me and I may remember, involve me and I learn."

— Benjamin Franklin

List your top 5 destinations for a field trip with your class.

(Imagine money is no object.)

1. ....

2. ....

3. ....

4. ....

5. ....

What skill or habit would you like to develop in the next year? How can you make time to develop it?

....

....

....

....

....

....

....

....

....

....

....

....

....

....

....

....

"Have no fear of perfection—you'll never reach it."
— Salvador Dalí

What is your favorite time of day? Why?

....

....

....

....

....

....

....

....

....

....

....

....

....

....

....

....

List 5 of your best personality traits.

1. ....

2. ....

3. ....

4. ....

5. ....

"Play is the highest form of research."

—Albert Einstein

List 5 ways you're going to make the most of your summer break.

1. ....

2. ....

3. ....

4. ....

5. ....

Monday	Tuesday	Wednesday	Thursday

Friday	Saturday	Sunday	January
			Notes

Friday	Saturday	Sunday	February
			Notes

Monday	Tuesday	Wednesday	Thursday

Notes

Monday	Tuesday	Wednesday	Thursday

Monday	Tuesday	Wednesday	Thursday

Friday	Saturday	Sunday	May
			Notes

Monday	Tuesday	Wednesday	Thursday

Friday	Saturday	Sunday	June
			Notes

Monday	Tuesday	Wednesday	Thursday

Friday	Saturday	Sunday	July
			Notes

Monday	Tuesday	Wednesday	Thursday

Friday	Saturday	Sunday	August
			Notes

Monday	Tuesday	Wednesday	Thursday

September

Notes

Monday	Tuesday	Wednesday	Thursday

Notes

Monday	Tuesday	Wednesday	Thursday

Friday	Saturday	Sunday	November
			Notes

Monday	Tuesday	Wednesday	Thursday

Friday	Saturday	Sunday	December
			Notes

Children's Books That Celebrate Teachers

❦ ❦ ❦

A Letter to My Teacher by Deborah Hopkinson, illustrated by Nancy Carpenter

Written as a thank-you note to a special teacher from the student who never forgot her, this moving story makes a great read-aloud.

The Art of Miss Chew by Patricia Polacco

This true story shows just how important a teacher can be in a child's life—and celebrates the power of art itself.

The Day You Begin by Jacqueline Woodson, illustrated by Rafael López

Jacqueline Woodson and Rafael López have teamed up to create a poignant, yet heartening book about finding courage to connect, even when you feel scared and alone.

Because of Mr. Terupt by Rob Buyea

Because of Mr. Terupt features seven narrators, each with a unique story, and each with a different perspective on what makes their teacher so special.

Wonder by R. J. Palacio

Over 6 million people have fallen in love with Wonder and Auggie Pullman, the ordinary boy with the extraordinary face, who inspired a movement to Choose Kind.

Recommended Books for Educators

𝄞 𝄞 𝄞

What Teachers Make: In Praise of the Greatest Job in the World by Taylor Mali

The right book at the right time: an impassioned defense of teachers and why we need them now more than ever.

The Bridge to Brilliance: How One Principal in a Tough Community Is Inspiring the World by Nadia Lopez and Rebecca Paley

Be inspired by the magnetic young principal who "stands on the front line of the fight to educate America's children" (Brandon Stanton, author of *Humans of New York*) and the book that *Essence* calls "Essential reading."

Teaching Hope: Stories from the Freedom Writer Teachers and Erin Gruwell by The Freedom Writers and Erin Gruwell

Teaching Hope unites the voices of the Freedom Writer teachers, who share uplifting, devastating, and poignant stories from their classrooms, stories that provide insight into the struggles and triumphs of education in all of its forms.

Reading with Patrick: A Teacher, a Student, and a Life-Changing Friendship by Michelle Kuo

A memoir of the life-changing friendship between an idealistic young teacher and her gifted student, jailed for murder in the Mississippi Delta

I Did My Homework in My Head (and Other Wacky Things Kids Say) by Alyssa Cowit and Greg Dunbar

Based on the hit Instagram @LivefromSnackTime, here are irresistible quotes from the elementary school classroom that prove kids really do say the darndest things.

Books to Motivate and Inspire

❧ ❧ ❧

Rising Strong: How the Ability to Reset Transforms the Way We Live, Love, Parent, and Lead by Brené Brown

Brown has listened as a range of people—from leaders in Fortune 500 companies and the military to artists, couples in long-term relationships, teachers, and parents—shared their stories of being brave, falling, and getting back up.

I've Been Thinking . . . Reflections, Prayers, and Meditations for a Meaningful Life by Maria Shriver

A book of reflections for those seeking wisdom, guidance, encouragement, and inspiration on the road to a meaningful life.

The Happiness Advantage: The Seven Principles of Positive Psychology That Fuel Success and Performance at Work by Shawn Achor

Using stories and case studies from his work with thousands of Fortune 500 executives in 42 countries, Achor explains how we can reprogram our brains to become more positive in order to gain a competitive edge at work.

Give and Take: Why Helping Others Drives Our Success by Adam Grant

A groundbreaking look at why our interactions with others hold the key to success, from the bestselling author of *Originals*.

The Power of Meaning: Finding Fulfillment in a World Obsessed with Happiness by Emily Esfahani Smith

Smith shows us how cultivating connections to others, identifying and working toward a purpose, telling stories about our place in the world, and seeking out mystery can immeasurably deepen our lives.

Big Magic: Creative Living Beyond Fear by Elizabeth Gilbert

From the worldwide bestselling author of *Eat Pray Love* and *City of Girls*: the path to the vibrant, fulfilling life you've dreamed of.

Made in the USA
Las Vegas, NV
10 May 2021